LEADING
THE WAY

THE TRUE GOSPEL AND HOW TO SHARE IT

A WORKBOOK COMPANION
FOR GROUP STUDY

DONALD E. JONES, PHD

J & A Book Publishers
www.jabookpublishers.com

ISBN-13: 978-1946368096
ISBN-10: 1946368091

DEDICATION

I dedicate this book to my Savior and Lord Jesus Christ. He has been with me every step of my journey upon the Earth, and I so look forward to being in His presence forever and ever.

CONTENTS

ACKNOWLEDGMENTS

I want to thank my wonderful and gracious wife Carol who has supported me in this ministry with sacrifice, enthusiasm, encouragement, and accountability. Most of all, she has been a constant blessing because of her willingness to listen. I was always sharing with her the truths God had been teaching me as I studied His word and wrote this book. It consumed many hours. Thank you, Carol and I deeply love you.

I want to thank my son Gregory R. Jones for volunteering to be the primary editor of this important book. Without his time and effort in painstakingly and meticulously going over every word and every sentence checking and rechecking the sentence structure and grammar, I would not have been able to complete it. Thank you for your ministry to me. I love you my son.

I want to thank my other children, Krista, Matt, and Kara for their love for Christ and His Word and their willingness to live for Him. I love you all.

Introduction

This workbook is designed to aid in the comprehension and application of the truths from the Scriptures which are found in the book of the same name. It has a question and answer format because asking questions was a powerful teaching method that the Lord used to reveal God's divine truth. Jesus asked over one hundred and thirty questions as He instructed the people of God and others. These are only the recorded ones. We can only speculate as to how many questions He might have actually asked. The Lord used His questioning techniques to prompt His listeners to focus, understand, analyze, evaluate, and apply the principles He was proclaiming to them. The same has been done in this workbook.

In John chapter six, through His healing ministry, the Lord Jesus had gathered a large crowd from the surrounding villages and towns who were following Him and fed over five thousand of them from a few loaves and fish in a boy's basket. The people were so astounded by the miracle that they thought they should take Jesus by force and make him king. As a result, Jesus left the crowd by Himself. The disciples took one of the boats and ventured across the Sea of Galilee at night. It was at this time Jesus walked in the water, was received into the boat, and it was immediately at the other side. When morning came the crowds found Him in the city of Capernaum having searched everywhere. John records their first question. In John 6:25, it says, "When they found him on the other side of the sea, they asked him, 'Rabbi, when did you come here?'"

Jesus knew what was in their hearts and acknowledged that they had come for more bread. He urged them to stop seeking the food for their bodies and instead the food for their souls which he could provide. They disregarded what Jesus declared and asked Him to bring bread out of heaven as the prophet Moses had done. They wanted their physical needs met, not their spiritual. When the Lord Jesus refused, they begged for the power to create their own physical bread.

Then, He claimed that they needed to believe in Him and receive eternal life. Utilizing the bread as an analogy, the Lord proclaimed that He was the "bread out of heaven" and they needed to eat His flesh and drink His blood (possess Him spiritually) to have eternal life. They thought they already possessed eternal life as Jews, why would they need to Him to be saved? They needed Him for a miracle. With this, some of his many followers (not the twelve) left.

Then, Jesus asks the first of two penetrating questions. In John 6:61, the apostle writes, "But Jesus knowing in himself that his disciples murmured at this, said to them, 'Does this cause you to stumble?'" He knew some had followed Him only for what they could receive from Him in this life (Judas is implied here also). Yet, this was not why He came. As many left, Jesus ask the next one to His disciples alone. In John 6:67-69, His question and their response is described, "Jesus said therefore to the twelve, 'You don't also want to go away, do you?' Simon Peter answered him, 'Lord, to whom would we go? You have the words of eternal life. We have come to believe and know that you are the Christ, the Son of the living God.'" Here, Peter shows they were true followers. They needed Him for His Words first.

Their confusion was not over the eating and drinking His blood but over eternal life coming only from Him. The Lord used questions to discover their belief. His questions helped them focus, understand, analyze, evaluate, and apply truth. May these do the same for you in this book.

Chapter 1

Know the Kingdom Plan

For Christians to share the gospel they must know and understand the kingdom plan. This includes the creation, fall, and redemption of all mankind.

In the section, "A Typical Scenario," the author describes how Christians can share the gospel with their neighbors who live near them.

What is the scenario about?

What held the believer back from sharing the gospel?

What finally led the Christian to share the good news and how did it occur?

Have you had a similar experience?

In the section, "A Scriptural Principle" the author presents an important biblical principle in evangelism which concerns our knowledge and understanding of God's kingdom plan.

How would you express this principle in your own words?

How would you rewrite this principle to make it even more personal to your life (using your name and situation)?

Why do you think this principle might be important in your life right now as you share the gospel?

How would you rate yourself on the percentage of times you followed this principle in the past as a believer?

Directions: Put a horizontal mark and your name where you see yourself on the percentage line.

| 0% | 25% | 50% | 75% | 100% |

In the section, "A Biblical Explanation," the author explains the gift of God's kingdom to His Son and its importance in sharing the gospel effectively.

What is the primary reason God, the Father, created human beings according to Romans 8:29-30?

What are three other reasons, God created people and what bible passages describe them?

After Adam and Eve sinned against God, what are some of the blessings (name two) that people could no longer enjoy (provide verses)?

After Adam and Eve sinned against God and came under His wrath, what was the result in this life and the next?

What greater blessings (name three) can people now enjoy because of God's plan of redemption (provide verses)?

In what ways might these truths impact your life?

In the section, "An Ancient Portrait," the author provides a unique portrayal of how one of the thieves hanging next to our Lord became a believer.

Can you briefly describe the setting of this real-life ancient drama?

Can you describe the major characters involved?

How did the evangelist initiate the gospel presentation?

What was result of this evangelistic presentation?

How was the principle explained in this chapter applied to the situation?

Based on the truths learned in this chapter, what would you have done differently if you were the evangelist or how would you have responded if you were the recipient?

In the section, "A Modern Anecdote," the author discusses a situation in which a woman in his bible study group needed assistance in sharing the gospel with her grandmother.

Can you briefly describe the setting of this real-life modern drama?

Can you describe the major characters involved?

How did the author initiate the gospel presentation?

What was result of this evangelistic presentation?

How was the principle explained in this chapter applied to the situation?

Based on the truths learned in this chapter, what would you have done differently if you were the author or how would you have responded if you were the recipient?

In the section, "A Personal Response," the author provides a model you may use for prayer if you find it necessary after discovering the truths in this chapter.

Are you presently attempting to present the gospel of Jesus to someone? If not, are there some in your immediate family who may not know Jesus Christ and may need prayer for an opportunity for you to share with them and open hearts to receive Him?

Based on the truths you have just learned, what will you continue to do in your current evangelistic efforts and what might you do differently?

What additional thoughts would you like to share with the others?

Chapter 2

Herald the Epic Message

For Christians to share the gospel, they must understand that they are messengers of a powerful declaration given by by God. They can witness anywhere, anytime, to anyone.

In the section, "A Typical Scenario," the author explains how the saints might begin a conversation about Christ in a local coffee shop they may frequent.

What is the scenario about?

What held the believer back from sharing the gospel?

What finally led the Christian to share the good news and how did it occur?

Have you had a similar experience?

In the section, "A Scriptural Principle" the author presents an important biblical principle in evangelism which concerns our right and responsibility to share the gospel.

How would you express this principle in your own words?

How would you rewrite this principle to make it even more personal to your life (using your name and situation)?

Why do you think this principle might be important in your life right now as you share the gospel?

How would you rate yourself on the percentage of times you followed this principle in the past as a believer?

Directions: Put a horizontal mark and your name where you see yourself on the percentage line.

0%	25%	50%	75%	100%

In the section, "A Biblical Explanation," the author explains our unique position as heralds of the King of Kings and its importance in sharing the gospel effectively.

What are the differences between "announcing" the plan and "preaching" the plan?

How does someone actually "comfort" with the message of the gospel?

What does it mean to "proclaim" the plan of redemption and give an example from the Bible?

What are the differences between "testifying" and "teaching" the plan of redemption?

How was the gospel message "delivered" to us and what are we supposed to do about it?

In what ways might these truths impact your life?

In the section, "An Ancient Portrait," the author provides a unique portrayal of an incident of mistaken identity when Paul shared the gospel.

Can you briefly describe the setting of this real-life ancient drama?

Can you describe the major characters involved?

How did the evangelist initiate the gospel presentation?

What was result of this evangelistic presentation?

How was the principle explained in this chapter applied to the situation?

Based on the truths learned in this chapter, what would you have done differently if you were the evangelist or how would you have responded if you were the recipient?

In the section, "A Modern Anecdote," the author discusses a situation in which he was able to present the good news to a woman who had come to his church in the past.

Can you briefly describe the setting of this real-life modern drama?

Can you describe the major characters involved?

How did the author initiate the gospel presentation?

What was result of this evangelistic presentation?

How was the principle explained in this chapter applied to the situation?

Based on the truths learned in this chapter, what would you have done differently if you were the author or how would you have responded if you were the recipient?

In the section, "A Personal Response," the author provides a model you may use for prayer if you find it necessary after discovering the truths in this chapter.

Are you presently attempting to present the gospel of Jesus to someone? If not, are there some in your extended family who may not know Jesus Christ and may need prayer for an opportunity for you to share with them and open hearts to receive Him?

Based on the truths you have just learned, what will you continue to do in your current evangelistic efforts and what might you do differently?

What additional thoughts would you like to share with the others?

Chapter 3

Accept the Divine Mandate

Christians have been given a divine mandate to share the gospel of the kingdom of God. This involves recognizing, accepting, and acting upon this critical spiritual command.

In the section, "A Typical Scenario," the author discusses how believers might respond to criticisms of Jesus Christ in their classroom by their teacher or fellow classmates.

What is the scenario about?

What held the believer back from sharing the gospel?

What finally led the Christian to share the good news and how did it occur?

Have you had a similar experience?

In the section, "A Scriptural Principle" the author presents an important biblical principle in evangelism which concerns our commission as divine emissaries of Jesus Christ.

How would you express this principle in your own words?

How would you rewrite this principle to make it even more personal to your life (using your name and situation)?

Why do you think this principle might be important in your life right now as you share the gospel?

How would you rate yourself on the percentage of times you followed this principle in the past as a believer?

Directions: Put a horizontal mark and your name where you see yourself on the percentage line.

0%	25%	50%	75%	100%

In the section, "A Biblical Explanation," the author explains the divine mandate that all believers have been given and its importance in sharing the gospel effectively.

In what ways do Christians glorify God in their presenting of the plan of redemption and unbelievers in their reaction to the plan presented?

What is the difference between God's "command" to share the good news and His "call" to do it?

What is the difference between our testimony about Jesus being a "characteristic" of our salvation and it being a result of our "spiritual maturity"?

What is God's divinely chosen method of evangelism and how is it to be accomplished?

What are two additional reasons Christians should present the gospel with the outside world (provide verses)?

In what ways might these truths impact your life?

In the section, "An Ancient Portrait," the author provides a unique portrayal of the salvation of the Ethiopian eunuch on the road to Gaza.

Can you briefly describe the setting of this real-life ancient drama?

Can you describe the major characters involved?

How did the evangelist initiate the gospel presentation?

What was result of this evangelistic presentation?

How was the principle explained in this chapter applied to the situation?

Based on the truths learned in this chapter, what would you have done differently if you were the evangelist or how would you have responded if you were the recipient?

In the section, "A Modern Anecdote," the author discusses a situation in which he was able to share the gospel with a set of triplets.

Can you briefly describe the setting of this real-life modern drama?

Can you describe the major characters involved?

How did the author initiate the gospel presentation?

What was result of this evangelistic presentation?

How was the principle explained in this chapter applied to the situation?

Based on the truths learned in this chapter, what would you have done differently if you were the author or how would you have responded if you were the recipient?

In the section, "A Personal Response," the author provides a model you may use for prayer if you find it necessary after discovering the truths in this chapter.

Are you presently attempting to present the gospel of Jesus to someone? If not, are there some in your neighborhood who may not know Jesus Christ and may need prayer for an opportunity for you to share with them and open hearts to receive Him?

Based on the truths you have just learned, what will you continue to do in your current evangelistic efforts and what might you do differently?

What additional thoughts would you like to share with the others?

Chapter 4

Allow God to Be Sovereign

As Christians proclaim the gospel, God is also at work. It takes a dynamic interaction between God and man to bring others to the gospel. In this chapter, we focus on God's role.

In the section, "A Typical Scenario," the author mentions ways in which believers might share their faith in Christ in the employee's lunchroom.

What is the scenario about?

What held the believer back from sharing the gospel?

What finally led the Christian to share the good news and how did it occur?

Have you had a similar experience?

In the section, "A Scriptural Principle" the author presents an important biblical principle in evangelism which concerns God's sovereign role in the sharing or the gospel.

How would you express this principle in your own words?

How would you rewrite this principle to make it even more personal to your life (using your name and situation)?

Why do you think this principle might be important in your life right now as you share the gospel?

How would you rate yourself on the percentage of times you followed this principle in the past as a believer?

Directions: Put a horizontal mark and your name where you see yourself on the percentage line.

| 0% | 25% | 50% | 75% | 100% |

In the section, "A Biblical Explanation," the author explains the Lord God's role in evangelism and the importance of this knowledge in sharing the gospel effectively.

In what different ways are the Father, the Son, and the Holy Spirit involved in the sharing of the gospel?

Who ultimately sends believers to share the gospel?

What promise can believers claim if they feel too inadequate to share the gospel and does this mean they will not need to be trained?

Why do we not have to worry about persuading people to open their hearts to God?

Does a Christian have to be concerned that if they missed an opportunity to share the gospel with people, they may never come to Christ?

In what ways might these truths impact your life?

In the section, "An Ancient Portrait," the author provides a unique portrayal of Saul's persecution of Christians and then his miraculous conversion to Christ.

Can you briefly describe the setting of this real-life ancient drama?

Can you describe the major characters involved?

How did the evangelist initiate the gospel presentation?

What was result of this evangelistic presentation?

How was the principle explained in this chapter applied to the situation?

Based on the truths learned in this chapter, what would you have done differently if you were the evangelist or how would you have responded if you were the recipient?

In the section, "A Modern Anecdote," the author discusses his own conversion to Jesus Christ as a young man ready for adulthood.

Can you briefly describe the setting of this real-life modern drama?

Can you describe the major characters involved?

How did the author initiate the gospel presentation?

What was result of this evangelistic presentation?

How was the principle explained in this chapter applied to the situation?

Based on the truths learned in this chapter, what would you have done differently if you were the author or how would you have responded if you were the recipient?

In the section, "A Personal Response," the author provides a model you may use for prayer if you find it necessary after discovering the truths in this chapter.

Are you presently attempting to present the gospel of Jesus to someone? If not, are there some among your many friends who may not know Jesus Christ and may need prayer for an opportunity for you to share with them and open hearts to receive Him?

Based on the truths you have just learned, what will you continue to do in your current evangelistic efforts and what might you do differently?

What additional thoughts would you like to share with the others?

Chapter 5

Allow Man to Be Challenged

Not only does God have a part in the proclamation of the plan but man also. In His infinite wisdom, God decided to use people to proclaim His plan to other people.

In the section, "A Typical Scenario," the author demonstrates how the followers of Jesus Christ can share the gospel with old high school friends at their reunions.

What is the scenario about?

What held the believer back from sharing the gospel?

What finally led the Christian to share the good news and how did it occur?

Have you had a similar experience?

In the section, "A Scriptural Principle" the author presents an important biblical principle in evangelism which concerns the believer's role in sharing the gospel.

How would you express this principle in your own words?

How would you rewrite this principle to make it even more personal to your life (using your name and situation)?

Why do you think this principle might be important in your life right now as you share the gospel?

How would you rate yourself on the percentage of times you followed this principle in the past as a believer?

Directions: Put a horizontal mark and your name where you see yourself on the percentage line.

| 0% | 25% | 50% | 75% | 100% |

In the section, "A Biblical Explanation," the author explains the role believers play in evangelism and their willingness to accept it and take action to share the gospel effectively.

What is a major obstacle that keeps Christians from sharing the gospel?

According to Acts 1:3, what two things did Jesus Christ do to prepare His disciples for ministry before his ascension?

According to Acts 2, who chose to share the gospel after the Spirit manifested the tongues of fire?

According to Acts 8:4, what did the Christians choose to do after they were scattered?

What is the main difference in evangelism between choosing an opportunity God provides and making one?

In what ways might these truths impact your life?

In the section, "An Ancient Portrait," the author provides a unique portrayal of Paul's sharing of the gospel with Sergius Paulus.

Can you briefly describe the setting of this real-life ancient drama?

Can you describe the major characters involved?

How did the evangelist initiate the gospel presentation?

What was result of this evangelistic presentation?

How was the principle explained in this chapter applied to the situation?

Based on the truths learned in this chapter, what would you have done differently if you were the evangelist or how would you have responded if you were the recipient?

In the section, "A Modern Anecdote," the author discusses a situation where he, as a pastor, met with a man who was dying in the hospital.

Can you briefly describe the setting of this real-life modern drama?

Can you describe the major characters involved?

How did the author initiate the gospel presentation?

What was result of this evangelistic presentation?

How was the principle explained in this chapter applied to the situation?

Based on the truths learned in this chapter, what would you have done differently if you were the author or how would you have responded if you were the recipient?

In the section, "A Personal Response," the author provides a model you may use for prayer if you find it necessary after discovering the truths in this chapter.

Are you presently attempting to present the gospel of Jesus to someone? If not, are there some among your classmates who may not know Jesus Christ and may need prayer for an opportunity for you to share with them and open hearts to receive Him?

Based on the truths you have just learned, what will you continue to do in your current evangelistic efforts and what might you do differently?

What additional thoughts would you like to share with the others?

Chapter 6

Persist in Watchful Prayer

Prayer is one of the most effective and powerful tools for bringing people to Christ. Believers should pray consistently and persistently for the unsaved.

In the section, "A Typical Scenario," the author shows how believers can share their Christian testimonies to the beloved members of their extended family.

What is the scenario about?

What held the believer back from sharing the gospel?

What finally led the Christian to share the good news and how did it occur?

Have you had a similar experience?

In the section, "A Scriptural Principle" the author presents an important biblical principle in evangelism which concerns the power of prayer as believers share the gospel.

How would you express this principle in your own words?

How would you rewrite this principle to make it even more personal to your life (using your name and situation)?

Why do you think this principle might be important in your life right now as you share the gospel?

How would you rate yourself on the percentage of times you followed this principle in the past as a believer?

Directions: Put a horizontal mark and your name where you see yourself on the percentage line.

0%	25%	50%	75%	100%

In the section, "A Biblical Explanation," the author explains how to move the hand of God in prayer and its importance in sharing the gospel effectively.

What are two examples in the Bible of the power of prayer?

Does God desire us to pray for the unsaved? Why or why not?

According to Mark 1:35, what was an essential part of the Lord's gospel ministry?

What are at least three reasons for prayer as Christians share the gospel?

What are at least three prayer requests as believers present God's plan of redemption?

In what ways might these truths impact your life?

In the section, "An Ancient Portrait," the author provides a unique portrayal of Paul's imprisonment in Philippi and what God was able to accomplish.

Can you briefly describe the setting of this real-life ancient drama?

Can you describe the major characters involved?

How did the evangelist initiate the gospel presentation?

What was result of this evangelistic presentation?

How was the principle explained in this chapter applied to the situation?

Based on the truths learned in this chapter, what would you have done differently if you were the evangelist or how would you have responded if you were the recipient?

In the section, "A Modern Anecdote," the author discusses a situation where he was able to proclaim the kingdom of God at a camp for teens.

Can you briefly describe the setting of this real-life modern drama?

Can you describe the major characters involved?

How did the author initiate the gospel presentation?

What was result of this evangelistic presentation?

How was the principle explained in this chapter applied to the situation?

Based on the truths learned in this chapter, what would you have done differently if you were the author or how would you have responded if you were the recipient?

In the section, "A Personal Response," the author provides a model you may use for prayer if you find it necessary after discovering the truths in this chapter.

Are you presently attempting to present the gospel of Jesus to someone? If not, are there some among your co-workers who may not know Jesus Christ and may need prayer for an opportunity for you to share with them and open hearts to receive Him?

Based on the truths you have just learned, what will you continue to do in your current evangelistic efforts and what might you do differently?

What additional thoughts would you like to share with the others?

Chapter 7

Proclaim the Proper Message

All people receive Jesus Christ through a clear and exact message of salvation proclaimed to them. This is a work of the Spirit not the persuasion of men.

In the section, "A Typical Scenario," the author presents an account of how the saints can testify of their faith during the Christmas season.

What is the scenario about?

What held the believer back from sharing the gospel?

What finally led the Christian to share the good news and how did it occur?

Have you had a similar experience?

In the section, "A Scriptural Principle" the author presents an important biblical principle in evangelism which concerns declaring the true gospel with all of its elements.

How would you express this principle in your own words?

How would you rewrite this principle to make it even more personal to your life (using your name and situation)?

Why do you think this principle might be important in your life right now as you share the gospel?

How would you rate yourself on the percentage of times you followed this principle in the past as a believer?

Directions: Put a horizontal mark and your name where you see yourself on the percentage line.

0%	25%	50%	75%	100%

In the section, "A Biblical Explanation," the author explains the elements of the plan of redemption and their importance in bringing true believers into the kingdom.

What are two New Testament examples of proclaiming sin and judgment in the gospel message?

What are two examples of the proclamation of Jesus as God by Jesus Himself and one of his apostles?

Briefly, what does it mean to proclaim Jesus as both "Savior" and "Lord?"

What three defenses for Christ's deity does the Holy Spirit utilize to bring people to Christ?

What are three terms used in the Bible that indicate receiving Jesus as Savior and Lord involves a relationship with Jesus not just a cursory knowledge of Him?

In what ways might these truths impact your life?

In the section, "An Ancient Portrait," the author provides a unique portrayal of Peter's encounter with a lame man on his way to the temple.

Can you briefly describe the setting of this real-life ancient drama?

Can you describe the major characters involved?

How did the evangelist initiate the gospel presentation?

What was result of this evangelistic presentation?

How was the principle explained in this chapter applied to the situation?

Based on the truths learned in this chapter, what would you have done differently if you were the evangelist or how would you have responded if you were the recipient?

In the section, "A Modern Anecdote," the author discusses how his four children received Jesus Christ as Savior and Lord in their early years.

Can you briefly describe the setting of this real-life modern drama?

Can you describe the major characters involved?

How did the author initiate the gospel presentation?

What was result of this evangelistic presentation?

How was the principle explained in this chapter applied to the situation?

Based on the truths learned in this chapter, what would you have done differently if you were the author or how would you have responded if you were the recipient?

In the section, "A Personal Response," the author provides a model you may use for prayer if you find it necessary after discovering the truths in this chapter.

Are you presently attempting to present the gospel of Jesus to someone? If not, are there some who may attend your local church who may not know Jesus Christ and may need prayer for an opportunity for you to share with them and open hearts to receive Him?

Based on the truths you have just learned, what will you continue to do in your current evangelistic efforts and what might you do differently?

What additional thoughts would you like to share with the others?

Chapter 8

Utilize Your Interests and Skills

Christians should develop evangelistic strategies which are performed alone or with other believers. They should be created around their particular interests, skills, and gifts.

In the section, "A Typical Scenario," the author portrays the ways Christians can share the gospel while participating in their favorite activities.

What is the scenario about?

What held the believer back from sharing the gospel?

What finally led the Christian to share the good news and how did it occur?

Have you had a similar experience?

In the section, "A Scriptural Principle" the author presents an important biblical principle in evangelism which concerns the development of personal evangelistic strategies.

How would you express this principle in your own words?

How would you rewrite this principle to make it even more personal to your life (using your name and situation)?

Why do you think this principle might be important in your life right now as you share the gospel?

How would you rate yourself on the percentage of times you followed this principle in the past as a believer?

Directions: Put a horizontal mark and your name where you see yourself on the percentage line.

| 0% | 25% | 50% | 75% | 100% |

In the section, "A Biblical Explanation," the author explains the building of personal evangelistic strategies around our background, interests, abilities, and gifts and its importance in sharing the gospel effectively.

.

What are three biblical examples of those who used personal evangelistic strategies and describe them?

How do spiritual gifts pertain to proclaiming the gospel?

What is an example of an individually tailored presentation of the gospel in the books of Acts?

What did Paul mean when he said he did not want to offend people as he shared the gospel? What did he not mean?

How do the members of the church as a whole testify to the world that they have a relationship with Christ?

In what ways might these truths impact your life?

In the section, "An Ancient Portrait," the author provides a unique portrayal of the Lord Jesus and His encounter with a Samaritan woman.

Can you briefly describe the setting of this real-life ancient drama?

Can you describe the major characters involved?

How did the evangelist initiate the gospel presentation?

What was result of this evangelistic presentation?

How was the principle explained in this chapter applied to the situation?

Based on the truths learned in this chapter, what would you have done differently if you were the evangelist or how would you have responded if you were the recipient?

In the section, "A Modern Anecdote," the author discusses a situation in which he decided to present the gospel during his college speech classes.

Can you briefly describe the setting of this real-life modern drama?

Can you describe the major characters involved?

How did the author initiate the gospel presentation?

What was result of this evangelistic presentation?

How was the principle explained in this chapter applied to the situation?

Based on the truths learned in this chapter, what would you have done differently if you were the author or how would you have responded if you were the recipient?

In the section, "A Personal Response," the author provides a model you may use for prayer if you find it necessary after discovering the truths in this chapter.

Are you presently attempting to present the gospel of Jesus to someone? If not, are there some who may be among your acquaintances who may not know Jesus Christ and may need prayer for an opportunity for you to share with them and open hearts to receive Him?

Based on the truths you have just learned, what will you continue to do in your current evangelistic efforts and what might you do differently?

What additional thoughts would you like to share with the others?

Chapter 9

Welcome an Initial Response

Moving from unbelief to belief may require some people to make initial steps toward the gospel without receiving Christ at the moment that His redemptive plan is presented.

In the section, "A Typical Scenario," the author provides an example for the saints to present the gospel by connecting to the individual interests of their immediate family members.

What is the scenario about?

What held the believer back from sharing the gospel?

What finally led the Christian to share the good news and how did it occur?

Have you had a similar experience?

In the section, "A Scriptural Principle" the author presents the numerous ways the people can positively respond to the gospel without making an immediate commitment to Christ.

How would you express this principle in your own words?

How would you rewrite this principle to make it even more personal to your life (using your name and situation)?

Why do you think this principle might be important in your life right now as you share the gospel?

How would you rate yourself on the percentage of times you followed this principle in the past as a believer?

Directions: Put a horizontal mark and your name where you see yourself on the percentage line.

0%	25%	50%	75%	100%

In the section, "A Biblical Explanation," the author explains the numerous initial positive responses to the gospel and their importance in sharing the good news effectively.

What are two biblical examples of those who made an initial response to Christ but did not yet believe in Him?

What is the difference between responding to the good news with an honest confusion and an open mind?

What is the difference between responding to the good news with a fearful awakening and a difficult opposition?

What is the difference between responding to the good news with a continued persuasion and continual presentation?

What must Christians do when unbelievers respond to the gospel desiring a scriptural consideration?

In what ways might these truths impact your life?

In the section, "An Ancient Portrait," the author provides a unique portrayal of a woman's tears at the feet on Jesus in the house of Simon.

Can you briefly describe the setting of this real-life ancient drama?

Can you describe the major characters involved?

How did the evangelist initiate the gospel presentation?

What was result of this evangelistic presentation?

How was the principle explained in this chapter applied to the situation?

Based on the truths learned in this chapter, what would you have done differently if you were the evangelist or how would you have responded if you were the recipient?

In the section, "A Modern Anecdote," the author discusses a situation where he challenged a friend to seriously compare the Bible with all other religious writings.

Can you briefly describe the setting of this real-life modern drama?

Can you describe the major characters involved?

How did the author initiate the gospel presentation?

What was result of this evangelistic presentation?

How was the principle explained in this chapter applied to the situation?

Based on the truths learned in this chapter, what would you have done differently if you were the author or how would you have responded if you were the recipient?

In the section, "A Personal Response," the author provides a model you may use for prayer if you find it necessary after discovering the truths in this chapter.

Are you presently attempting to present the gospel of Jesus to someone? If not, are there some among your teammates who may not know Jesus Christ and may need prayer for an opportunity for you to share with them and open hearts to receive Him?

Based on the truths you have just learned, what will you continue to do in your current evangelistic efforts and what might you do differently?

What additional thoughts would you like to share with the others?

Chapter 10

Pursue a Saving Faith

In evangelism, Christians must pursue a true saving faith as a response to the gospel. This is not merely words but a belief and a trust that literally changes people's lives.

In the section, "A Typical Scenario," the author identifies how Christians might determine if the people they might want to date may be believers.

What is the scenario about?

What held the believer back from sharing the gospel?

What finally led the Christian to share the good news and how did it occur?

Have you had a similar experience?

In the section, "A Scriptural Principle" the author presents an important biblical principle in evangelism which concerns the true response that saves.

How would you express this principle in your own words?

How would you rewrite this principle to make it even more personal to your life (using your name and situation)?

Why do you think this principle might be important in your life right now as you share the gospel?

How would you rate yourself on the percentage of times you followed this principle in the past when you did something wrong in a relationship?

Directions: Put a horizontal mark and your name where you see yourself on the percentage line.

| 0% | 25% | 50% | 75% | 100% |

In the section, "A Biblical Explanation," the author explains the elements of the proper response to the gospel and their importance in sharing the gospel effectively.

What are the three aspects involved in one truly repenting of his or her sin to receive Christ?

What does it really mean to "believe" in Jesus?

What does it really mean to "receive" Jesus as Savior?

How does one's initial "submission" to Christ as Lord impact his or her future life?

If faith alone saves, what is its relationship to good works?

In what ways might these truths impact your life?

In the section, "An Ancient Portrait," the author provides a unique portrayal of Paul's ministry among the many people of Ephesus.

Can you briefly describe the setting of this real-life ancient drama?

Can you describe the major characters involved?

How did the evangelist initiate the gospel presentation?

What was result of this evangelistic presentation?

How was the principle explained in this chapter applied to the situation?

Based on the truths learned in this chapter, what would you have done differently if you were the evangelist or how would you have responded if you were the recipient?

In the section, "A Modern Anecdote," the author discusses a situation concerning the response of the good news by two young ladies at a vacation bible school.

Can you briefly describe the setting of this real-life modern drama?

Can you describe the major characters involved?

How did the author initiate the gospel presentation?

What was result of this evangelistic presentation?

How was the principle explained in this chapter applied to the situation?

Based on the truths learned in this chapter, what would you have done differently if you were the author or how would you have responded if you were the recipient?

In the section, "A Personal Response," the author provides a model you may use for prayer if you find it necessary after discovering the truths in this chapter.

Are you presently attempting to present the gospel of Jesus to someone? If not, are there some who may be members of a local club you belong to who may not know Jesus Christ and may need prayer for an opportunity for you to share with them and open hearts to receive Him?

Based on the truths you have just learned, what will you continue to do in your current evangelistic efforts and what might you do differently?

What additional thoughts would you like to share with the others?

Chapter 11

Expect a Dramatic Reaction

When people receive Jesus as Savior and Lord, some will respond immediately and dramatically while others may react slowly and meticulously.

In the section, "A Typical Scenario," the author depicts the support a Christian gives his sister when she has a dramatic reaction to receiving Christ.

What is the scenario about?

What held the believer back from sharing the gospel?

What finally led the Christian to share the good news and how did it occur?

Have you had a similar experience?

In the section, "A Scriptural Principle" the author presents an important biblical principle in evangelism which concerns the dramatic reactions of some who receive Christ.

How would you express this principle in your own words?

How would you rewrite this principle to make it even more personal to your life (using your name and situation)?

Why do you think this principle might be important in your life right now as you share the gospel?

How would you rate yourself on the percentage of times you followed this principle in the past as a believer?

Directions: Put a horizontal mark and your name where you see yourself on the percentage line.

0%	25%	50%	75%	100%

In the section, "A Biblical Explanation," the author explains the ways in which new believers may demonstrate their new faith and its importance in sharing the gospel effectively.

Do all people who receive Christ as Savior and Lord have a dramatic reaction? Why or why not?

What is the difference between the responses of tremendous sense of blessing and a great feeling of joy?

How can the response of a wonderful willingness to suffer be related to an overwhelming desire to evangelize?

How might a strong devotion to the proclaimer relate to an immediate participation in ministry?

What is the relationship between a removal of things from the old life and a dramatic transformation?

In what ways might these truths impact your life?

In the section, "An Ancient Portrait," the author provides a unique portrayal of the dramatic reaction of the chief tax-collector Zacchaeus when he came to Christ.

Can you briefly describe the setting of this real-life ancient drama?

Can you describe the major characters involved?

How did the evangelist initiate the gospel presentation?

What was result of this evangelistic presentation?

How was the principle explained in this chapter applied to the situation?

Based on the truths learned in this chapter, what would you have done differently if you were the evangelist or how would you have responded if you were the recipient?

In the section, "A Modern Anecdote," the author discusses a situation in which he was able to present the good news of Jesus Christ to an old high school friend from drama club.

Can you briefly describe the setting of this real-life modern drama?

Can you describe the major characters involved?

How did the author initiate the gospel presentation?

What was result of this evangelistic presentation?

How was the principle explained in this chapter applied to the situation?

Based on the truths learned in this chapter, what would you have done differently if you were the author or how would you have responded if you were the recipient?

In the section, "A Personal Response," the author provides a model you may use for prayer if you find it necessary after discovering the truths in this chapter.

Are you presently attempting to present the gospel of Jesus to someone? If not, are there some who frequent a favorite place of yours who may not know Jesus Christ and may need prayer for an opportunity for you to share with them and open hearts to receive Him?

Based on the truths you have just learned, what will you continue to do in your current evangelistic efforts and what might you do differently?

What additional thoughts would you like to share with the others?

Chapter 12

Counter with a Loving Attitude

As Christians share the good news, people may respond in a negative manner. Believers should be careful to react in a way that reflects the character of God.

In the section, "A Typical Scenario," the author depicts the loving reaction of a believer to the gospel presentation he gave to someone he helped on the road.

What is the scenario about?

What held the believer back from sharing the gospel?

What finally led the Christian to share the good news and how did it occur?

Have you had a similar experience?

In the section, "A Scriptural Principle" the author presents an important biblical principle in evangelism which concerns the loving reactions of believers to rejections of the gospel.

How would you express this principle in your own words?

How would you rewrite this principle to make it even more personal to your life (using your name and situation)?

Why do you think this principle might be important in your life right now as you share the gospel?

How would you rate yourself on the percentage of times you followed this principle in the past as a believer?

Directions: Put a horizontal mark and your name where you see yourself on the percentage line.

| 0% | 25% | 50% | 75% | 100% |

In the section, "A Biblical Explanation," the author explains the attitudes Christians should have to negative reactions to the gospel and its importance in sharing it effectively.

If the saints don't take revenge on those who persecute them, then who will?

What does it mean to "love" those who persecute us?

What kind of blessings do we give those who persecute us and why?

What prayer requests should we offer to God for those who persecute us and why?

If we are not to resist persecutors, then what circumstances would this encompass?

In what ways might these truths impact your life?

In the section, "An Ancient Portrait," the author provides a unique portrayal of the encounter of the Lord Jesus with the rich young ruler.

Can you briefly describe the setting of this real-life ancient drama?

Can you describe the major characters involved?

How did the evangelist initiate the gospel presentation?

What was result of this evangelistic presentation?

How was the principle explained in this chapter applied to the situation?

Based on the truths learned in this chapter, what would you have done differently if you were the evangelist or how would you have responded if you were the recipient?

In the section, "A Modern Anecdote," the author discusses a situation in which he recruited a group of Christians who were trained in evangelism to work with his club program.

Can you briefly describe the setting of this real-life modern drama?

Can you describe the major characters involved?

How did the author initiate the gospel presentation?

What was result of this evangelistic presentation?

How was the principle explained in this chapter applied to the situation?

Based on the truths learned in this chapter, what would you have done differently if you were the author or how would you have responded if you were the recipient?

In the section, "A Personal Response," the author provides a model you may use for prayer if you find it necessary after discovering the truths in this chapter.

Are you presently attempting to present the gospel of Jesus to someone? If not, are there some who might serve you regularly at a store who may not know Jesus Christ and may need prayer for an opportunity for you to share with them and open hearts to receive Him?

Based on the truths you have just learned, what will you continue to do in your current evangelistic efforts and what might you do differently?

What additional thoughts would you like to share with the others?

Chapter 13

Disciple with a Serious Intent

Once unbelievers receive Jesus Christ as their Savior and Lord, it does not end there. Someone will have to help these new believers navigate their new lives in Christ.

In the section, "A Typical Scenario," the author displays the ways Christians can follow up conversations that they may have begun with people they casually meet.

What is the scenario about?

What held the believer back from sharing the gospel?

What finally led the Christian to share the good news and how did it occur?

Have you had a similar experience?

In the section, "A Scriptural Principle" the author presents an important biblical principle in evangelism which concerns how to disciple or build up new believers in their faith.

How would you express this principle in your own words?

How would you rewrite this principle to make it even more personal to your life (using your name and situation)?

Why do you think this principle might be important in your life right now as you share the gospel?

How would you rate yourself on the percentage of times you followed this principle in the past as a believer?

Directions: Put a horizontal mark and your name where you see yourself on the percentage line.

| 0% | 25% | 50% | 75% | 100% |

In the section, "A Biblical Explanation," the author explains how we are to assist new believers in their growth in Christ and its importance in sharing the gospel effectively.

What are they to really concentrate on in their Christian lives and why?

What are two ways they can individually grow in Christ and explain each briefly?

What are two ways they can grow in Christ that involves the saints in a local church?

What are two ways they can grow in Christ that involves those who do not know Christ as Savior and Lord?

What must they commit themselves to do to live righteously and how do they deal with sins and trials that will come?

In what ways might these truths impact your life?

In the section, "An Ancient Portrait," the author provides a unique portrayal of Paul's discipleship of a master and his runaway slave.

Can you briefly describe the setting of this real-life ancient drama?

Can you describe the major characters involved?

How did the evangelist initiate the gospel presentation?

What was result of this evangelistic presentation?

How was the principle explained in this chapter applied to the situation?

Based on the truths learned in this chapter, what would you have done differently if you were the evangelist or how would you have responded if you were the recipient?

In the section, "A Modern Anecdote," the author discusses a situation where he visited a couple who desired to become new members of his church but were not saved.

Can you briefly describe the setting of this real-life modern drama?

Can you describe the major characters involved?

How did the author initiate the gospel presentation?

What was result of this evangelistic presentation?

How was the principle explained in this chapter applied to the situation?

Based on the truths learned in this chapter, what would you have done differently if you were the author or how would you have responded if you were the recipient?

In the section, "A Personal Response," the author provides a model you may use for prayer if you find it necessary after discovering the truths in this chapter.

Are you presently attempting to present the gospel of Jesus to someone? If not, are there some among those you may know from the past or on social media who may not know Jesus Christ and may need prayer for an opportunity for you to share with them and open hearts to receive Him?

Based on the truths you have just learned, what will you continue to do in your current evangelistic efforts and what might you do differently?

What additional thoughts would you like to share with the others?

Conclusion

As we conclude this book, I would like to leave us with some final thoughts about our God of salvation and what His Son did on the cross for us. First, if you read these books and realized that you have never received Christ as Lord and Savior, then I would like to provide that opportunity. If you are ready to receive Him, you can pray this prayer:

Dear God,

I want to be a part of your Son's kingdom. I know that all I deserve is judgment for my sin. I am so sorry for what I have done. I believe Jesus is your Son. I know this because he resurrected from the dead. I believe that He died on the cross to pay the penalty for my sin. I believe that He is the only way to heaven. I welcome and receive Him into my life right now as Savior. I turn my life over to Him as Lord and Master. I want a love relationship with Jesus Christ. I thank you for the blessings you are bestowing on me right now. I am grateful for my entrance into heaven which was gained by the faith your Spirit gave me and not by any works. I will do my best to live for you and fulfill the purpose for which I have been created.

If you prayed that prayer and meant it then the Holy Spirit has entered you and you are now a child of God. You must find yourself a bible teaching church and begin your adventure. If you reject these truths, God will always be waiting even until the day of your death. Please be warned that once death comes, then comes judgment. In Hebrews 9:27, the author warns all, "In as much as it is appointed for men to die once, and after this, judgment." I leave you with the most well-known verse in the world. It is John 3:16, "For

God so loved the world, that he gave his one and only Son, that whoever believes in him should not perish, but have eternal life." I hope I will see you in heaven!

Second, if you are a believer, you must go out into the world and tell people about the gospel you have just studied. You now have the tools to make a full and clear gospel presentation. Go share the good news of Jesus with the world!

ABOUT THE AUTHOR

Dr. Donald Jones is currently a Christian Pastoral Counselor with thirty-eight years of experience in the fields of pastoral ministry, public education, and Christian counseling. He carries degrees and certificates from four major universities and from a variety of educational institutions. He has been a professor of Languages and Bible, a television commentator, and a featured speaker at a variety of events and seminars at churches, schools, and other organizations across the United States. He is a member in good standing of several secular and Christian professional organizations. Dr. Jones has been a published author since 1976. For further information view his website at www.donjonesphd.com.

www.ingramcontent.com/pod-product-compliance
Lightning Source LLC
Chambersburg PA
CBHW021210020426
42331CB00003B/285